KINSHIP

POEMS EXPLORING BELONGING

KINSHIP

POEMS EXPLORING BELONGING

RENARD PRESS

RENARD PRESS LTD

124 City Road
London EC1V 2NX
United Kingdom
info@renardpress.com
020 8050 2928

www.renardpress.com

Kinship first published by Renard Press Ltd in 2023

Poems and biographies © the poets and judges, 2023
All other text © Renard Press, 2023

Cover design by Will Dady

Printed in the United Kingdom by Severn

ISBN: 978-1-80447-073-2

9 8 7 6 5 4 3 2 1

The poets assert their right to be identified as the authors of this work in accordance with the Copyright, Designs and Patents Act 1988.

CLIMATE POSITIVE Renard Press is proud to be a climate positive publisher, removing more carbon from the air than we emit and planting a small forest. For more information see renardpress.com/eco.

All rights reserved. This publication may not be reproduced, stored in a retrieval system or transmitted, in any form or by any means – electronic, mechanical, photocopying, recording or otherwise – without the prior permission of the publisher.

CONTENTS

About Kinship	11
About the Judges	12
Kinship	15
HISTORY BAKED IN A HOT OVEN *Caroline Bracken*	17
CARRIED *Dianne McPhelim*	19
A MEMOIRIST ASKS WHAT DESERT I WILL HAVE TO ENTER TO TELL MY STORY *Ivy Raff*	21
A RETURN *Michèle Clement*	23
A THREE-FOOT-WIDE DREAM *Anne Marie Wells*	25
AT I A.M. ON THE 6TH OF MARCH *Connor Johnston*	29
BAD INDIAN *Srishti Jain*	33

BEAUTIFUL APOSTATE *Bek King*	35
BIRTHRIGHT *Jessie Lee*	37
BLOOD ORANGE *Caoimhe Matthews*	39
BREAKING GROUND *Jean Gillespie*	41
CAN YOU SPELL THAT FOR ME? *Roisín Harkin*	43
CARBON SLOWLY TURNING *Steve Baggs*	45
CHAIN OF SUPPLY *Benedict Hangiriza*	49
DOMESTIC BLISS *Ilisha Thiru Purcell*	51
DOUBLE ENGLISH *Stuart Wrigley*	53
DOWN TO THE SEA AT MALAGA *Rosalie Alston*	55
DROP IN *Thea Smiley*	57
EARTHSTRUCK *Junyi Chew*	59
ELEGY FOR GREAT AUNT TRUDY *Renee Emerson*	61

FABLE *Naoise Gale*	63
FAMILY TREES *Daphne Sampson*	65
GENERATIONAL TRAUMA *Inga Piotrowska*	69
HADES *Elizabeth Train-Brown*	71
HERE'S TO US SPANGLISH KIDS *M.A. Dubbs*	73
HIRAETH *Sam Szanto*	75
HIS SHOES *Deborah Gaudin*	77
I THINK I MIGHT BE HUMAN *Kay Saunders*	79
JOURNEYMAN *Oz Hardwick*	81
LAST SUPPER 1993 *Mariyam Karolia*	83
LAUNDRY LITANY *A.W. Earl*	85
LETTERFALL *Utsuk Upreti*	87
LOVESONG *Alyson Smith*	89

MA, YOUR LITTLE GIRL IS BECOMING A PLANET *Fedora Mensah*	91
OHANA *Ellie Herda-Grimwood*	95
OUR FAMILY SCRAPBOOK *Erin Gannon*	101
REBEL YELL *Jazz McCoull*	105
SITTING ON A BENCH, WAITING *Steve Denehan*	107
SITTING ON YOUR BED *Ginger*	109
STYX *Jayant Kashyap*	113
TEETH REMOVAL CAN BE FUN, SOMETIMES *Rush Day*	115
THE OLD MAN AND THE VIOLIN *Catherine Edmunds*	117
THE SINGER *Niam Moore*	119
WE PICTURED IT SUNNY *Naomi Dean*	121
WHEN YOU WERE (BEFORE I WAS) *Vijaya Venkatesan*	123
XUĚLÓU, HÉNÁN 2021 *Mea Andrews*	125

YOU (A PUDDLE) 127
Tom Chachewitz

About the Poets 129
Supporters 144

ABOUT KINSHIP

In February 2021 Renard put out a call for submissions for the New Beginnings poetry project, a competition open to all those who 'felt their voice was silenced in 2020'. We were absolutely overwhelmed by the response to the project, and it became clear how important such open calls are for raising the voices of those who feel shut out of the mainstream.

The following year, building on this success, we launched the Spectrum project, seeking poems celebrating identity. We were, again, bowled over by the response.

This year we were delighted to announce the Kinship project, the resulting extraordinary anthology of which you hold in your hands, which seeks to build on these themes of identity and citizenship and to discuss notions of belonging.

As with any project, there were several vital people working away behind the scenes. Miriam Halahmy, Tom Denbigh (who must be credited with the great title), Reshma Ruia and Will Dady, the judges, had quite a task whittling down the list to the collection you see here today. Thanks, too, to Hannah Fields, a firm friend of these projects, for her support to date.

This project was supported by a crowdfunding campaign – thanks in abundance go to all those kind souls who supported the project; their names can be found on p. 144. And finally, our thanks to you, reader, for picking up this book, for supporting this project and, above all, for helping us to celebrate our great networks of belonging and identity.

THE PUBLISHER

ABOUT THE JUDGES

MIRIAM HALAHMY

Miriam was a teacher for twenty-five years, and, having worked with refugees and asylum seekers in schools, her writing engages with historical and contemporary issues that affect children across time – most notably the plight of refugees. Her young-adult novel, *Hidden*, was a *Sunday Times* Children's Book of the Week, was nominated for the Carnegie Medal and has been adapted for the stage. *A Boy From Baghdad*, Miriam's latest book, is about a boy who is forced into exile to Israel in 1951, with the entire ancient Iraqi Jewish community and the struggle to make a new life in a refugee camp.

TOM DENBIGH

Tom Denbigh is a Bristol-based poet and playwright. Exploring the queer experience alongside tales of friends and strangers, Tom's writing toys with myth, devilish humour and absurdity to portray the bizarre and brilliant in the everyday. He is a producer at Milk Poetry, a BBC1Xtra Words First winner and has facilitated writing workshops for groups of students from the UK and abroad. Outside of poetry Tom has a PhD on plant roots and soil erosion. His first collection *...and then she ate him* is published with Burning Eye Books.

ABOUT THE JUDGES

RESHMA RUIA

Reshma Ruia is an award-winning author and poet. She has a PhD and Master's in Creative Writing from Manchester University. She has published two novels (including *Still Lives* with Renard Press), a poetry collection and a short story collection. Her work has appeared in international anthologies and journals, and she has had work commissioned by the BBC. She is the co-founder of The Whole Kahani – a writers' collective of British South Asian writers. Born in India and brought up in Rome, her writing explores the preoccupations of those who possess a multiple sense of belonging.

WILL DADY

Will Dady grew up in the wonderfully named Great Snoring in North Norfolk, and now lives in London. He is the Publisher at Renard Press, which he founded in 2020. A publisher of classic and contemporary fiction, non-fiction, theatre and poetry, part of Renard's raison d'être is to empower and provide a platform to marginalised voices. The New Beginnings project was set up in 2021, followed by Spectrum in 2022; the huge success in attracting stirring entries has made these projects a firm fixture in Renard's publishing programme.

KINSHIP

WINNER
HISTORY BAKED IN A HOT OVEN
Caroline Bracken

RUNNER-UP
CARRIED
Dianne McPhelim

SPECIAL MENTIONS FROM THE JUDGES

MIRIAM HALAHMY
AT 1 A.M. ON THE 6TH OF MARCH
Connor Johnston

TOM DENBIGH
A THREE-FOOT-WIDE DREAM
Anne Marie Wells

RESHMA RUIA
A MEMOIRIST ASKS WHAT DESERT I WILL
HAVE TO ENTER TO TELL MY STORY
Ivy Raff

WILL DADY
STYX
Jayant Kashyap

HISTORY BAKED IN A HOT OVEN

Caroline Bracken

My Granda cursed your Granda
when yours burst into Boland's Mills,
Howth rifle cocked, looking for trouble.

Mine was elbow deep in dough,
two hours in to a twelve-hour shift;
he'd no time for them Rialto boyos.

Six years later mine was stopped
in the bread van at an arms check
on Sackville Street, recognised the soldier

pointing a gun at him as yours: Alright John?
Yours waved him on – that was his mistake:
more than yeast rising in them loaves.

My uncle a twelve-year-old apprentice,
silent in the passenger seat, he'd already mastered
the art of giving nothing away.

KINSHIP

They say I have the look of him.

When we met none of this was spoken.
When we parted we didn't throw our family
histories in each other's faces –

already had enough of our own.

One hundred years on from the Civil War
our son is in the kitchen; he's taken a figary
to bake cinnamon rolls,

mixing and kneading like a pro.
He bides his time, waits for the dough
to rest and rise until the final proof

and it's ready for him to wield the rolling pin.
At his first attempt they are perfect,
just the right amount of give.

Some inclinations are in the blood.

CARRIED

Dianne McPhelim

Carry me.
Fat fists punch the air, demanding
your eyes squint against the sun
I sigh, awkwardly scoop you, though my arms are full
up on my shoulders, your fingers uncurl
grasping my nostrils/hair/ears
pudgy knees squeeze my neck
sticky hands slap my forehead, cover my eyes
you say Mama look

Carry me.
Dramatically you slump to the ground
wrench and throw your shoes
inappropriate and new
blistered skin peeling
like the deflated balloons
you refuse to take down weeks after your birthday
socks stuck to heels and bloody
you say Mummy look

KINSHIP

Carry me.
You whisper at four am
gripping the wall
I hold back your hair
as you purge a poker hand of jacks
your head on sports wash, stomach on spin
drawing hatchet from the heart
gather splinters and rage
you say Mum look

Carry her.
Proudly offer your new world
a contended cloud
I recognise this stranger
peach fuzzed with pert chin
arms stretch in slumber, fists fighting air
dimples frame a first thin-lipped smile
we catch our breath
you say Nanna look

Carry me.
I say, hollow bones in sensible shoes and layers
knees and mind grinding
my world small and puckered
like a wool jumper from a hot wash
recognising you as the woman who reads the news
you sigh and tuck your head against mine
above us, swallows are returning
you say Mother look

A MEMOIRIST ASKS WHAT DESERT I WILL HAVE TO ENTER TO TELL MY STORY

Ivy Raff

Desert of the tsar. Desert of pogrom. Desert of Atlantic.
Of grandmother in ground, of grandmother in hold of ship,
of grandmother's clandestine marriage and kitchen-table
abortions. Desert of Brighton Beach. Desert of Williamsburg.
Desert of Bedford Stuyvesant after Desert of Houston Street after
Desert of borders then-unexisted, scrubbed from Desert
of Empire. Desert of the wandered-out Jew: butchers
and tailors and timber merchants. Desert of shoulders
forever compressed, of wrists torqued back. Desert of hip,
of nerve endings, of nerves unending, of nerves beginning.
Desert of factory fires, of picket lines, of fighting for wages
and workweeks, of tenements rat-clawed. Desert of egg breads in braids,
of brined fish in jars, eyeless, matzo-plumped. Desert of soup,
and soup, and soup again. Of celery. Of beets. Of chicken bones
stretched for marrow-days. Of chicken fat rendered, roasting
pan-harvested, plopped in a jar atop the icebox. No butter
in the desert, just schmaltz already heat-proofed.

KINSHIP

To tell my story the desert must die and move to the suburbs.
Must choose wallpaper from swatches in great hardcover sample books
while fluorescence hums overhead. To tell my story I must
forget bitter herbs, forget Yiddish poems, unsing songs. Unchant. Unbleed.
Unsubmit. Nonchalant. Relearn womanness. Reassemble
chopped lettuce into whole, crisp leaves. I must forget pants
and wrap myself homespun. I must enter
others' deserts alone: Gobi, Mojave, Sahara, Sonora.
My own Desert died, lady. My Desert drowned
in the Atlantic.

A RETURN

Michèle Clement

I plod, shroud-heavy, through the cold grounds.
I stop, arrested by a familiar heady aroma.
In a bed by the path, a red geranium.
I rub its fleshy leaves,
bring my thumb and forefinger to my nose,
find the hook on which a memory hangs.
It feels far from this rhododendron-bright,
alien boarding school where I am the newest flower,
a dying blossom.

I fly, dream-light, to my lantana lair.
I lie, nestled in the soft, warm, ochre earth
with its spicy smell, tinged with the sea.
Around me are the iridescent pink, yellow,
magenta of the lantana flowers. The scent
overwhelms me: citrus, herby, exotic,
tropical. I listen to the sounds from the kitchen:
the scouring of the pans, the familiar sway of Swahili.
And I am home at last.

Anne Marie Wells

A THREE-FOOT-WIDE DREAM

-catcher ensnared a bull elk,
his 800-pound heft noosed,

antlers lassoed to his ankles
by the rope burrowing deeper

into his bloody tendons
with every desperate thrust

of himself at himself, or at no one
or at the ground, or at God. Because of

some idiot's Pinterest-inspired backyard
decor, he lay like a hostage, like

his limbs were the stems of a bride
's bouquet, as if he were a pig ready

for the spit to carry him to the roast

KINSHIP

until a man approached,
a faceless man. I was the man,

I mean, it felt like I was this man
as he closed in on the beast,

GoPro strapped to his chest, knife outstretched.
He grabbed the pitiful creature by the bone branch

-ing from his skull, swiped his blade across the tethers
until they splintered apart, flaying each thread until

the animal could writhe himself free, blood
painting his legs in bands and streams.

I wonder still how that elk understood
the intervention that saved his life. If his

understanding runs parallel to my own
after inexplicable luck, if there couldn't be

altruistic beings beyond my comprehension
of the universe and beyond what I know life to be

and what it is not, beyond who I know
to be beast and who is not. Have I ever

walked away from a tragic fate limping,
not knowing someone, something released

the binds that would have starved me to death,
without knowing what a knife was or a man,

not knowing to say thank you, or maybe
not even knowing I had been rescued at all.

Maybe they keep rescuing me anyway,
posting their good deeds for others to watch,

for others to write poems about what they saw.

AT 1 A.M. ON THE 6TH OF MARCH

AFTER AUDITIONING FOR A PLAY ATTACHED TO THE OPENING OF A QUEER HISTORY EXHIBITION, AND THEN GOING ON A DATE, AND THEN ANXIOUSLY TIDYING MY ROOM

Connor Johnston

That queerness is a fast-track friendship
Became clear to me as we instinctively
Asked for each other's Instagram tags,
As if we still had the blood on our hands
From botched surgeries and bricks thrown
By those for whom the act of finding family
Was the very lifeblood that kept them alive.

It's true that we cannot pass down blood;
It is not in our nature. Instead we imbue objects
With magic, we call them parts of ourselves,
Decorate whole museums with our effigies,
Totems, and live immortally amongst the art,
Throughout the ages, bloodlessly and pretty.

And as we laid out the things in our bags
As part of the audition's 'ice breaker'
We saw our souls' constellations,

KINSHIP

And knew that a life and a community
Can be described as a bag of sundries
That mean something in their sum.

We knew that only five of us would get in,
But when the audition ended, we were
Together allied against an unfair world.
Now I think of those numbers in my phone
As checkpoints, anchors, back-up plans
And safety nets in which to catch myself,

Because the world is so much better now,
But we have warned ourselves against hope.
Rough-hewn diamonds toughened
By the heavy lifting of a soul into the light
Against so much weight and resistance
That most of us are still pushing instinctively.

I hope too much that I get the part.
I hope so much that my heart hurt
When I saw his huge brown eyes
And wide beaming smile in the shape
Of a blanket cut from the cloth
Of the first and most perfect Warmth.

Too many things are at once true:
He listened too attentively, too lovingly,
His jokes were too funny, our unique
Energies too compatible, too affable,
Too full of light were the Capri-Suns
We sipped in Westgate discussing

AT 1 A.M. ON THE 6TH OF MARCH

How to reject the law of non-contradiction,
How to only sort of want kids and marriage,
How to thrive in a moment and manage
To be every potential at once until you act.
And then he kisses me, and the hope in me
Is too large and too happy, and I kiss back.

My room is a mess, my head is everywhere,
I half-tidy it into a bundle and stare at it there.
I realise I cannot let him see this room, not yet.
I still need to vacuum the floor and buy
Some hyacinths, sunflowers, lavender tufts
And green carnations to feel at home here.

I've hardly decorated this uni room
With the boiler buzzing and the walls white
But for scant postcards and some book piles.
When I left home I thought I would carve myself
Like marble and appear suddenly, all fresh
And beautiful, fixed, for ever, perfection.

Texting him, I realise my room is in my phone,
Giggling past midnight, my face blue
And my eyes square and my heart warm.
I realise I am lucky, and I have decorated
My notes app, where I keep my poetry,
And my contacts, where I keep my family.

BAD INDIAN

Srishti Jain

Mother says not to make it political
– why don't you write like Neruda, whom I read
in my youth and loved
and believed in love
through him? Mom, Neruda was a rapist,
and this poetry
writes me, really.
Really, who has the luxury any more, of
believing in love, or the audacity,
when the earth is burning? And
everyone is blaming
the fire on the infidels. if only we burnt
away the infidels. It seems otherness
sells, and so does delusion, and all the good
people of this land think the way out of the fire
is by burning those people.
Hence, it must be so. If you think about it,
it's a masterstroke,
really; to make everyone feel unIndian,
ungodly, unworthy of birth or land.
To unbelong one from oneself with a chasm so deep

KINSHIP

so as to dissect them –
unless they pick a sword
and slit, instead, those people that dare
to live and look different
or love different or, god forbid,
pray different. Mother, I swear,
I sat down to write about a love I felt once
which was so true, but how could it remain apolitical
when truth is revolt? So tonight, I can write
the saddest lines – I am no longer
in recognition or belonging of this land
of Azad, or this faith, and when
all of us are burning together, and our arms
carry saffron embers over etchings of those people,
we will go to our respective heavens
or angels or rebirths,
and shout soundlessly into endless skies
just how good we were.

BEAUTIFUL APOSTATE

Bek King

My mother is a daughter.

Sometimes I forget she gave me this Promethean voice.
That it grew inside her, once, like a tangerine,
Ready to ripen and shake the glass of my father's walls,
With a Sapphic tongue,
        before it would be later halved and given away.

Sometimes her lips shut tight with absence.
Between each exhale of her Cupid's bow hangs the letter 'I',
Petrifying itself like a splinter.

We are shaped from clay,
By hands given to those once shaped,
And when my mother belonged to her mother, a ring
Was misplaced somewhere around her left rib.
Metal that wore her from her left hand,
After she climbed down her own throat to retrieve it −
        back when she belonged to God.

KINSHIP

Those born in church are born with their strings
Planted atop their heads like inverted roots, growing upwards,
Clawing for the sun,
        Having never known the leaf.

At thirty-eight my mother cut her strings,
And did so by cutting a finger from her left hand.
To heal, she touched her lips to forbidden fruits,
Although it did not so much as heal, but numb
What feeling was felt for her friends,
Now falling through her —
        Just as her mother did, at the end of the mirage.

She was left, with us:
Four clay daughters,
And her lover,
        To which they say God still shakes his head.

But warmth is deserved.
Stolen for us by a true prophet,
Who knew the price of his motherhood,
Just as a mother knows the price of life;
Unlike the gods, who do not know what it means to live,
Or what it means to be made.

God will never feel how gently
                      the morning star
Kisses our dying flesh;

Just as two women kiss
When they're seeing the colour green for the very first time.

BIRTHRIGHT

For my mother, who has made sure I am proud of my skin.

Jessie Lee

you want to hear about something authentic?
here's my birth story.
here's generations of history
mapped out on my face, tunnelled into my skin.
this isn't just my face.
this is my culture's. this is my mother's,
and her mother's, and her mother's.
and every time you make a passing joke about it,
you are using a barbed wire
to cut into my foundations.
i want to tell you every beautiful thing
that my people have ever done for this world,
but the words die on the way to my lips
like a funeral march.
why do i need to prove that we are worthy of being respected?
is my being here not enough?
these eyes, this nose, this hair, this skin…
can you not see these centuries
being moulded to show the world proudly?

KINSHIP

this is all hard work and fingers in the dirt.
my mother has two tongues
living in her mouth in fluent harmony.
i have spent my entire life in this country,
and i have tried to balance it with my heritage somewhere else.
here's a hammer and here's a nail;
i give you permission to crack me open
and witness the war inside my brain.
maybe that'll help you understand.
look there, you'll be able to see that some days
i feel guilty for being ashamed to speak my own language,
inheritance blurred somewhere along the way.
look there, i have tried to shape myself
to look more like you.
why are you still here? i have told you:
here's generations of history mapped out on my face,
and i am done trying to cover it.
why am i still battling my way to show these two sides of me?
stop hammering now.
my body has taken enough abuse for being a body.
for being my home.
how's this for something authentic?

BLOOD ORANGE

Caoimhe Matthews

The taxi driver said I am blessed by God. That He will give me a round, fresh son. Because of the frozen cat in bin bags in the back seat.

I just wish for God to point a finger and for the cat to shed the water it drowned in. Forget the other bag it was tied in. For the frost to glitter from its whiskers. I want her to mew and scratch and bite to escape.

I don't know her name, but she loved and was loved. This small being who knew joy and such terror in the end. Her people will be told today that she was stolen and spent her last moments in the river. That she was left to rot on the bank. They'll see the fly eggs in her blue eyes.

I want God to feel my hand as I reach it out to her. I want life to flow back into her broken frame. Instead of leaving me with a dead cat and a dead son.

BREAKING GROUND

Jean Gillespie

Some days when the water is low you can see the tips
of rooftops glistening under ripples, glimpse fish dart down
dark cobbled lanes, catch shadows searching out light
smears from sooty mouldering terraces.

Some days when the water is low you can see
frilled naked newts clinging to waving weeds
and delicate grasses growing along those ghostly
cloistered ways. You can listen to a choir of larks
rise on trilling notes, a song of buoyed feathers
threaded on light rising spires, an act of faith.

high   higher   highest

Some days when the water is low I think of my
grandfather lying beneath those sparkling waters,
his life force spent spooning earth into little heaps,
anthills of dry brittle extract that rose to become
scaly and monstrous, each spoonful a ragged
earth-tooth, raw and discarded.

KINSHIP

bit　　　　by　　　　bit　　　　by　　　　bit

Some days I think of the children who, with me, once
trampled up through the slag, scrambling ankle deep
in the flakes of ore to reach a high point, only to slide
down on bits of old discarded lino with whooping cries
to doleful men who hacked the earth for a living,
down into sunken emptied pockets.

Some days I stand looking at those waters
and think of my grandfather in a cloth cap,
who twisted round too late to see the looseness
of the overhanging rock. Who was born
too early to see the dawn rise golden through
the bullrush, too early to hear the smooth
mellow whoop of the curlew as it settles in the
long meadow grasses.

CAN YOU SPELL THAT FOR ME?

Roisín Harkin

'Can you spell that for me?' they'll ask.
Without thinking my lips move and out comes
The well versed, often rehearsed phonetic spelling
Of my first name, rolled off in a tempo that
Has slowed considerably since I first arrived here.
'R' for Romeo, 'O' for Oscar…

'The edges have come off your accent,' they'll say
When I return home for a family wedding
Or a friend's birthday, when they'll joke,
'Since when did we call it "Pry-Mark"?'
The weight of national identity lost
On those who never left.

CARBON SLOWLY TURNING

Steve Baggs

We turn slowly in our beds,
unaware of the geological.
The rocks, the carbon, the granite.
We understand so little.

The trees, the mountains,
we are moments, but we are.
The beach, the sea water, holding us,
swimming over us in light years.

My childhood was where
the chalk cliffs began.
All the years of erosion.
The mathematics of pebbles.

From the coast I can see
the dinghies crossing.
The blindness of our prejudices,
the handwritten slurs.

KINSHIP

There is more that unites us
than divides us. Remember that.
What are my roots? Homo habilis.
I ventured out of Africa.

Where I end, I begin;
The circle of life retreats.
There is a higher knowledge,
So trust in a kiss.

On Valentine's Day I pull you
from the boat.
A smile can translate
in any language.

Yes, you will have to see London to believe it.
Immense, giddy, confusing, a complication of
    traffic, transport and geography.
Out of the prison window
there are still stars.

Think now of all your silences.
The empty spaces between us.
The things we didn't say.
The interventions we didn't make.

Still, the long dark sleep of the soul
cannot stop the movement for change.
And the Earth is still laughing flowers.
And the planets are kissing in the sky.

CARBON SLOWLY TURNING

The fertility of love, the bluebell woods,
the coppiced trees, repeating the rhythms of life.
A part of everything, the great geometry,
the churn of timelessness.

Nature won't classify us –
we are more than a passport photo.
In this frozen time I am blur,
I am carbon, haematite, granite, slate.

I am millennia, I am a distant star,
I am my mother, I am my father.
What is my nationality?
I am human. I can still hold your hand.

We are here. We are boxers, artists,
tango-dancers, athletes, nurses.
What use is friendship
without friends?

The important things in life
are invisible to us.
Our thoughts, our spirits
cannot be buried.

We understand so little.
The rocks, the carbon, the granite.
Unaware of the geological,
we turn slowly in our beds.

CHAIN OF SUPPLY

Benedict Hangiriza

'Geological past shapes biological present.'
BLAKE DE PASTINO

sun-charred pits bloated with
bodies, sacks of bright-turquoise
shales. This biblical toil is all that
remains for progress's expanding
mouth. Each phone a remote
gulag, each battery emaciated limbs
atomised to electrolyte. Here eats young
and old, mother in close-ups returns to girl,
returns before miscarriages, before her
father's blood writhes a
cleft palate down the family tree to this
malleable, coltish frame of hills peppered
with bones like acres of rotting
fruit. Here the immovable shroud of conflict, the
    kind a *féticheur*'s ear refuses its charged cochlea,
    scours this land like the innards of a lokole
    drum. East and south and north and west
    rename this stalling country an alias of

slavery. Here alluvial-churned ghosts nudge us
    forward, backward where a sophist
representative denies the corpse
tally of dozens that find no bottom and empty into the
pliocene awaiting them as 35,000 grunts osmose
chests threaded with stick and straw.

DOMESTIC BLISS

For E.

Ilisha Thiru Purcell

We are mugs in a crowded cupboard,
clinking against each other
as our curves and hard edges seek new alignments.

In here, there is only space for us and our two names;
every other word loosens its grip,
love refracting into every nook and cranny.

Each time I choose you and you me
and we clink crockery
the stain of their fingerprints is sponged off,
until all that's left is not worth this ink.

Alone we have been through high fire
but with each turn of the moon our glaze deepens;
together
we are full to the brim.

DOUBLE ENGLISH

Stuart Wrigley

Coffee, fresh from the pot, made us feel older.
We followed Mr Sykes' sincere New England voice
Around the borders and shrubberies of Shakespeare and Pope.
The parallaxes of our voices align now
When I read that poetry.

Fragrant meaning still overwhelms.
'I sing – This verse to Caryll, Muse! is due'
Loses not its nutmeg Connecticut cadence.
It caressed and nurtured our reading, pruning and clipping.
I don't recall much now: his tie, his beard, his Citroën

And that sad scent of percolating coffee,
Brewing that dusty, fearless classroom,
A room filled with life,
Life not yet lived out
Of all its astonishing futures.

DOWN TO THE SEA AT MALAGA

Rosalie Alston

Last week I found a miniature jug
so you could still drink tea
in tiny gulps; now you've stopped drinking
your voice is slipping too, but you write
the word corporate today – you can't say
such a long word but you can still write it –
I love your resistance to set ways of doing things.

The hospice is bringing you a hospital bed today.
Your daughter is unwavering – her love is the star.

You have a wave of adventurism, decide
to clamber down your steep stairs,
hospital equipment sticking out of you, so
we can sit in the garden with ragged geraniums.

Now I have to talk about our cycle trip –
do you remember how we sauntered through
Spanish white villages, all the way from Granada
down to the sea at Malaga?

KINSHIP

I smile and you try to (your face is frozen), recalling
neither of us ever knew how to mend a puncture.

One of the best things I've ever done,
I say, and you nod and whisper,
One of the best things I've ever done too.

DROP IN

Thea Smiley

Catch me singing.
Appear in the hallway
clutching eggs in an old egg box,
or a newspaper clipping.

Or duck beneath the honeysuckle
through the side-gate to the garden,
and make me jump
as I'm hanging out the washing.

Let's talk about the books
we're reading,
or about the cat leaving half a rabbit
outside the back door,

or the swallows nesting in the garage
and pooing on the car,
or the last sighting of a barn owl
and where it might be living,

KINSHIP

or your trip to the coast
to photograph the starlings,
or where you hope to go
next winter.

Then, pluck a handful of fresh mint
from the front garden
as you walk to your car,
and I'll shout from the door:

Bye, Dad. See you later.

EARTHSTRUCK

Junyi Chew

In forty five minutes the sun rises
in forty five minutes the sun sets

orbiting this dark horizon
where even edges open out their innards

remember the Little Prince how he'd edge
back a chair on his tiny planet to watch the sun

sink again and again
tugging his sparrow heart toward the underworld

did I tell you about the first time
I saw our Earth from space

it was weightlessness that kept me
from falling to my knees in weeping

how I knew then in every cell of my body
I was part of her marbled beauty

KINSHIP

how sorry for the legions of moments
spent unmoored within her surfaces

when I return I will kiss the soil
like Odysseus on recognising his native Ithaca

I will sprinkle my husband's pillow with magnolia
and whisper in the morning air

a thousand gratitudes
for this one protean home

ELEGY FOR GREAT AUNT TRUDY

Renee Emerson

My favourite at the Roberson-Pruitt
reunions, she was famous for snagging
fur coats and jewels at local goodwills.

Hair teased up, a blonde cotton candy,
she smelled just as sweet. Her kitten heels
sank in the front-yard crabgrass, her lipstick
marked a smile of red on the rim of her glass
of iced tea, sweating in the Memphis summer.

She was the only one who didn't cast us off
like a stained shirt or three-legged chair
when my parents split. I hadn't seen her in years
when she was listed with all the dead kin
in a phone call with my mother about all
that was good about where we came from.

FABLE

Naoise Gale

Once upon a time, my mother tried to kill me.
They called it unreality, bent my brain
into a crossbow, folded each thought
like an anxious napkin. Tattooed my charts
with paranoia: held my arms. I wriggled

like an earthworm caught under fluorescence.
They told me bad girls get eaten,
consumed by corridors and endless white.
I watched the shape of my mother pacing a new,
sane solar system in front of me.

The schizophrenic storyteller chanted
from across the hall, voice of bleach
and mercy. She said bad girls get
swallowed, chewed, spat on. She said bad
girls get their cheeks pressed to

gravel and their bodies broken
under moonlight. She said bad girls who are
good girls who are mad girls get
lied about, get drugged. I pressed my

fists to my ears, hid under the chair, faux-
steel. I swallowed pink pills with stale water
and listened to the shush of my bad-girl heart:
she's killing you killing you killing you.

The ECG monitor bleeped like an omen,
Another bad girl smiled without her eyes.
I froze, thought for a moment, fear
an alarm clock. Trying to decide between
danger or danger or danger.

FAMILY TREES

Daphne Sampson

'Trees are presence.'
WENDELL BERRY

My childhood garden –
at the far end a huge sequoiadendron,
an Edwardian planter's folly,
lifted straight from Californian Redwood forests.
Taller than our three-floored house,
but not too proud to hold our swing.
Maybe its alien, spongy rust-red bark
helped cushion my little sister
when she, swinging too high, flew off.

The next, a monkey puzzle,
the garden comedian,
the mere thought of climbing a joke –
each branch armoured,
encased in scalpel-sharp leaves,
the central stems just brittle twigs.
Its very name calling the exotic colobus
to come and caper
in commuter-belt Kent.

KINSHIP

Nearer the house, a pine,
its thicket of small branches, some left sharply sawn,
forming a ladder, not to heaven
but, if rebellious, to dizzying heights
above my parents' window.
My nose to the bark, a resinous smell
an ooze of gluey syrup
to roll between fingertips like silver modelling clay,
looking sweet enough to eat, a gulab jamun.
So no surprise
when we find small flies and tiny wasps stuck
in amber.
Maybe I was moulding resin when I lost hold,
catching my thigh on one of the bayonet snags.

Stitched up royally, I was fine to climb again –
not the pine, but my best friend,
the beech.
Her cool grey bark smoother on my hands,
side branches huge anacondas, easy to straddle.
Its foliage in spring so vivid,
as if a giant had lifted the lawn towards the sun,
rendering it translucent,
in autumn this gown exchanged
for a marmalade gold taffeta.

One beech in the back garden, the other in the front,
alongside a large-leaved red turkey oak.

A teenager once lying lazy, prone while others gardened,
I willed myself to place
in a lasting box of memories

not the theory of complementary colours, possible O level
> revision,
but simply how that electric blue October sky shocked,
sent a high-voltage spark
into the tinder of red-gold leaves.

Last a Himalayan cedar,
a deodar,
her colour, needles and habit
softer than her cousin, the Christmas tree.
Boughs like draperies caressing and wrapping her children.
When I was four, Dad and I
dug its hole, drenched its roots,
inhaling its Christmas magic.

That tree last seen thirty foot tall,
framing the elderly couple,
frail from an all-night packing marathon:
my parents, for a while as sad to leave their garden
as I to migrate from their nest.

On recent drives
I failed to find it.
'Trees are presence.'
This one: an absence.

GENERATIONAL TRAUMA

Inga Piotrowska

I recently learned
you can't wash blood off marble,
and there are still Warsaw houses
with red-stained floors.

Apparently only prayer works.
If you say Our Father enough times,
end with a loud Amen,
you stop looking down.

After some time
the prayer becomes a shopping list,
work-meeting agenda,
tomorrow's date.

But no matter how many rosaries,
promotions or lovers,
blood won't come off marble.

In you lives
your grandma, raped by a Russian soldier,
grandpa, who was forced to look.

KINSHIP

As weeks go by,
stains become brighter
and you feel heavier, sadder.

You can't wash yourself off marble.

HADES

Elizabeth Train-Brown

They're talking about us, Hades, down in the village.
They're wondering why I keep visiting the god
in the wood, the dark king with a crown of bone
and sceptre of root. They keep saying the same thing –
She won't last the winter. She's not made for frost.
They think I'm climbing the rungs of your ribs into
my own grave. They think I'm sleeping with skeletons.
They think you're the reason my lips turn blue in church
and my fingers turn purple at the knuckle when I say
my Hail Marys. They've never had the stomach for you,
gem. They dug up your earth too fast, rinsed it
for the diamonds of your tears, grew fat and happy.
They don't like it when I ring my eyes with coal
like yours. They don't like it when I call you darling and
beloved and tender and dear. They don't like it.
And, sweet, I don't know what to do because, see,
these are my people, the way each chip of rock and
pebble of earth are yours. I've tried folding myself under
the foundations of my house, but the soil is no place for me.
I try to tell them that you love me warm, that you love
skating your hands over the hot expanse of my back,

kissing the heat from my neck, burying your nose
in the folds of my belly. But they still remember the way
your face appeared between two cloves of shadow
and took their loved ones somewhere they can't reach.

HERE'S TO US SPANGLISH KIDS

M.A. Dubbs

I see you fellow Spanglish kids,
see you doing a lateral jump in and out of worlds,
dipping toes but knowing you can't fully submerge.

Maybe you know enough Spanish to kinda get by,
get pulled by co-workers for a crude translation,
but not fluent to know all the words to bisabuela's favourite song
or always keep up in get-togethers.

I know your side-step, switch into masks and roles,
like we're some kind of Hombre Murciélago.
One day it's homemade tamales with tía
and the next it's Jell-O salad with your gran.
Every grannie's food is always fire.

Una día es Día de los Muertos a la ofrenda y luego
the next is Fourth of July and you're blowing up big shit in
    your cul-de-sac
like you're the real Uncle Sam and it's 1776.

KINSHIP

A toast to all of you and the beauty of balance,
even when the world wants us to sit on a side,
pick a bleacher for which team to root for.
On the days when you don't feel ____ enough,
and I know you have them,
know that you will always be Spanglish enough.

Spanglish isn't being half of this or part of another,
it's not fragments of culture broken into us.
It's pieces of ancestors forming a collage,
a unique mosaic with light shining through all the parts.
It's about being whole and complete,
exactly as we are.

So here's to you, my Spanglish kin!
Para ti. ¡Ahora y siempre!

HIRAETH

Sam Szanto

There is another place
                    in which she exists
              the girl I did not give birth to
                  fourteen years ago
now
                  she doesn't know my living children
                    my husband is a stranger to her
she spends half the summer away from me
        in winter her father comes uneasy to England
her grandparents fill a box with eggs
                  each September she appears with the leaves
                      in February she is in my heart's cold chambers
her home is me
              her home was me

HIS SHOES

Deborah Gaudin

He saw the abandoned shoe
and stepped backward, a boy again,
walking in his borrowed shoes.
Felt the indentation of his brother's
heel, the angry stamp of the toddler
he never outgrew.

He saw the shoe
and took a step back on the pavement,
though underfoot he smelt wet grass,
crushed its stalks and the roll
of small stones contoured him back
to a warm meadow.

He saw the shoe
and stepped back to boot the ball,
sending his shoe flying in a perfect
parabola against the blue,
in a time when all goals seemed
to be obtainable.

KINSHIP

He saw the shoe
and stepped back to remember,
under a scarred desk, their placed
companionship, his spit
and polish giving them a soft
school shine.

He saw his bare feet,
times it was his brother's turn,
shuffled in the copper-beech shade
shod in dapple and last year's fallen.
Then he was kingly in the wonder of his
elfin shoes.

He saw the shoe,
and all the steps of the footprints
that had walked him here, to this blue-
hazed morning, where the abandoned shoe
waited for him to place the other shoe
beside it.

I THINK I MIGHT BE HUMAN

Kay Saunders

I remember small laughter bouncing off red brick, a slip n'
 slide, my side red and yours blue,
I remember barbecues and smoke in the air, bandanas, sticky
 foreheads, tears, bugs,
A black dog stretched out, the clack of her claws.
I remember metal stools with black leather seats that wobbled,
The four of us crowded around a breakfast bar, TV too close,
 elbows bumping, ice cream from the freezer outside.
Everything was okay.
A sweet cupboard, cup cupboard, fridge next to the oven,
A chalkboard wall, flipflops by the backdoor, black countertops.
I remember that place with foggy certainty, and what a time to
 be human it was, what a time to flourish.

As I withstand the drudgery of my work
And gaze out the window between baskets and fuel
I think of my afternoon,
The songs I'll listen to on the way home, and what I'll eat.
Everything is okay.
People with thick bodies and a tummy that peaks out under
 their shirt buying snacks,
Old men who have glasses, the children that cradle their
 slushies to their chest and

KINSHIP

The women with bright nails or hair,
Teenagers that smile at me, boys with pink faces, girls who don't mind when our fingers brush,
The old regular who lit up when I complimented his haircut and the one who learnt my name.
They make a mistake, get embarrassed, I feel love bloom in my chest –
What a day to be human, I think, what a day to flourish.

I'll stare at apricot sunsets and comment on the steady chill in the air,
My wife will tuck the ends of her fingers inside her sleeves, my hand will be on the back of her neck.
The cats will call for dinner, the corgi's tail will thud on the wooden floor and there'll be two pigeons on the roof.
My wife will call them lovers.
We'll eat pasta with bread and talk about the recipe,
    giggle after one glass of wine.
Everything will be okay.
The kitchen sink will be full, and so will our bellies; my legs will be shaved and hers not;
The candle on our dresser will be too small to light and I'll promise to replace it tomorrow,
After dusting the bookshelves and making sure the living-room rug is straight, sitting on the porch, dancing in the hallway, singing to the countertops, piling oranges in the fruit bowl, baking, washing my hair, sewing up a hole in the sweater she wore the night before.
I will be messy and happy and unbridled; there will be a 'one-ness'.
And how it will feel to be human, oh, how it will feel to flourish.

JOURNEYMAN

Oz Hardwick

One day I saw my father wearing the costume of a clown; not as a metaphor for hidden sadness, but simply to keep the rain off. In his left hand he carried the tools of his trade: saws, screwdrivers, bright shillings, light bulbs, laughing gas and ladders – such bounty and beauty for a small, stiff hand. In his right hand he carried a glistening fish, strung from a silver thread. The fish's eyes were still alive, sparkling with punchlines and promises of a feast fit for dockside cats. That's all, that's all: we both heard the call of the circus, of the sea, and of my mother in her blue shoes and loose-fitting cardigan; and I ran like the breeze, but Dad ran with such perfect ease in those huge clown boots that all I could see was dust. We never mentioned this meeting. He taught me his trade, though the details faded and I learned new gestures that even I can barely understand. This is not a metaphor for finding my father in a different costume behind every word that I think's my own, but when I throw that reckless paint pot full in the faces of my modest crowd, a million silver fishes flutter like a child's dream of snow.

LAST SUPPER 1993

Mariyam Karolia

In the end I chose cheesy mash potato with baked beans,
whilst you wolfed down meat feasts and doner kebabs,
and a small cake brought out with a card.
A final night before this dead woman walked
to the electric chair of a prepayment meter,
never allowed to return.
In the end I crashed my clothes in bin liners
and you shook them out to fold,
geometrically perfect folds that said
no matter where you go
we hope you will find eudaimonia,
though you could never utter the words.
In the end we remembered introductions beneath a sky
made of crimson and Tyrian dyes,
as we were imprisoned for our parent's crimes.
In the end it was teaching you to read
when you taught me to play pool,
teaching you to sew,
cos you taught me to cook
cheesy mash potato… with baked beans.
In the end it was setting off the fire alarm

to fly into the grotesque night of distorted faces
and movies we were too young to watch.
In the end it was holding your hand
to stop you cutting your arms, your legs,
your heart right out of yourself,
and telling you again and again
that it wasn't your fault
when I didn't believe the words for myself.
In the end it was sharing stories,
family stories that would never be found on the Hallmark channel,
and finding strength in one another,
belief in one another,
wanting the best for one another
cos we were all we had.
In the end we were united by traumas unimaginable,
where no one remembers us
until another crime is committed
and those that care for us are blamed
for the crime they didn't commit.
In the end blood isn't thicker than water,
and I love you can be a lie.
In the end we all have twenty-seven bones in hands
still reaching out, hoping they won't be brushed away.

LAUNDRY LITANY

A. W. Earl

Take the corners, fold the sheets
we bought you for your second birthday
because
we were poor, because
the having of a grown-up bed
was gift enough, and fold
the valance sheet we got by mistake
but were too tired, too busy,
too shamefaced to replace,
and remind myself that your white socks have butterflies,
your sister's ones are plain.

This is a litany known
to no other mind, the thousand tiny
acts of care, measured out
in shirt sizes, in jean waists,
in just how much you've grown.
I learned adulthood on the job,
measured out my life in laundry days,
and now I know
which things are yours –

KINSHIP

the dresses, jumpers, skirts —
watch them come down the line,
remembering a thousand pegs,
a thousand frost-touched days,
the nappies I would fold before
putting them away, the clothes that did you both.
For years, your jeans hung
on the clothes horse's very lowest rung.
Now, sometimes, I think your things are mine.
One day you will be gone.
The loads will be smaller, just
the lonely things of empty nests.

This knowledge lives in me, will die with me,
this whose is whose, and when, and how,
and knowing in my very soul
that your white socks had butterflies,
that your sister's ones were plain.

LETTERFALL

Utsuk Upreti

Letters written by the dead to their living kin
fall from the sky just before the year's first snowfall.
We call it 'Letterfall'. It is the day my brother Dev
listens to his parents. I too receive their letters.

They died together, our parents. In our old house.
We were in the same house. But the fire was my pal and
we together hated them. I couldn't stop the fire, no, but I
could have asked my pal

to let them go, just like it let go of my brother. But
I didn't. I've stopped reading the letters from my
parents, though they write me every letterfall. Their
letters are piled up in my room like their memories –

both incombustible. I've tried many times to burn
the letters. Unlike their bodies, they don't. And I can
hear them breathe, laugh, cry and scream. Just like
them, I can't bear the letters. But what could I do?

KINSHIP

I asked the fire

to let me burn them just once. Just enough to make them
stop breathing, laughing, crying and screaming.
But it too is helpless. It said so, writing with flames on the
walls. 'Sorry, pal. You can't start a fire in the afterlife.'

LOVESONG

Alyson Smith

And soon he'll say
'It's our turn'
And I will push myself upon his back
And inhale the smell from the tweed and the ointment
That calms his skin
Which then
In turn
Calms me

MA, YOUR LITTLE GIRL IS BECOMING A PLANET

Fedora Mensah

NASA tells me a planet must do three things: it must orbit a star; it must be big enough for gravity to stretch it into a sphere; and it must be big enough for gravity to clear any similar-sized objects near its orbit.

Don't laugh at me, Ma, but I think your little girl is becoming a planet.
Her sparkling stretchmarks, like the skin of Saturn, weren't there yesterday.
Her red-hot temper and heart hardened with ice are new additions.
Ma, she's sweltering and expanding as we speak; she will outgrow your shoebox of a home.

Your little girl orbits you, Ma; honour and glory adorn your character.
For you are self-luminous, rotating at the centre of the small galaxy you call home.

KINSHIP

You crossed shimmering seas for a better life. You learnt a new language at the expense of your dignity, squinting at small italics in an English textbook under the glow of a broken lamplight.

Your little girl faces dilemmas you won't understand;
    the kinds 'good girls' shouldn't face;
These western therapists, call one of them a

hedgehog's dilemma:
'A situation in which a group of hedgehogs seek to move close to one another to share heat during cold weather. They must remain apart, however, as they cannot avoid hurting one another with their sharp spines.'

Ma, do you not see your daughter's spines?
They grow from her hands, her waist and her feet.
It's becoming harder for her to walk, harder to run from men who crouch like dogs at her feet, waiting to pounce.
Have you forgotten that our society has loosened the leashes
    on these men?
Have you forgotten that they are free to roam and prey on
    daughters like yours?

Ma, don't you feel your daughter's spine? Look at your stomach now. You don't feel the grip of her thorn or see the shapes of Mars-size blood marks on your Kente clothes? What about the smear of blood on your face, and on hers?

Don't laugh at me, Ma, but your little girl is becoming a
    planet.

MA, YOUR LITTLE GIRL IS BECOMING A PLANET

For now she has stretched into a sphere, and she'll soon clear you from her orbit and drown you in the beauty of a black hole – a fall from grace and into dreamy awe.

What would your church sisters say? Picture their haunting laughter as you and your daughter fade from pictures and into shocking oblivion. Your fall from renown will for ever be remembered – it will become a folk tale that will outlive you, a tale for the ages, a new chapter in a history book.

boa no, Ma,
help her, Ma.

                Let her go, let her grow, Ma.
                Only you can save her now.
                For holding her is hurting you.

OHANA

Ellie Herda-Grimwood

Welcome to Kaua'i, where the valleys green are lush
and the beauty of the mountains bring about a solemn hush
as the ocean waves gush and your legs the chickens brush
as they enjoy the landscape plush and the lack of city crush.

You're on the garden island (where you've always wanted to go)
and yet your stomach starts to drop as your feet begin to slow.
Incoming in-laws, happy and smiling, come on, smile back like a pro.
Your social anxiety's improved – 'you've got this' – your confidence
    has grown.

But the thoughts start to spiral (as they oh so often do).
'Why would they be pleased?' They're here for your wife, not for you.
So you consider backing away as your negativity starts to stew,
and your thoughts go into overdrive as they cunningly accrue.

But after all that worry and fretting that you'll never truly belong,
the cuddles make swift work of you, unassuming and strong.
The timidity you thought had guaranteed eternal exile from the throng
has been totally ignored and now you know your fear was wrong.

KINSHIP

Your lovely sister says warmly that it is '*so* good to see you',
and her partner with excellent sideburns (since last time they definitely grew)
both pull you in for hugs so tight, they feel most overdue,
and so the vacation begins in the Hawaiian sun with a blended family brew.

Your nice teenage nephew's sprouted up like a taaaalllll beanpole,
and your baby nephew is beautiful, the sweetest little soul.
The middle nephews, in they run to get big hugs from your wife;
the little one's unalarmed by you but the elder's suspicion is rife.

Your younger sister states heartily that she's glad we all made it here,
her husband's reaction is slower but he's glad to see us, it's clear.
Your brother doesn't come in for a hug but that's OK, we're both shy,
he seems genuinely happy to see us both, so perhaps a hug later, we'll try.

Finally in comes the matriarch (your throat goes dry), your mother-in-law,
over she comes, and you lunge in to embrace, trying to feel just a little secure,
but she hugs you back and you immediately feel all right, calm and mature;
so here you are, amongst your clan, fully safe and reassured.

What follows is a holiday unlike any other –
you feel a part of everything, one thing after another.
The wise old honu drifting in to rest upon the sand,
you sit and watch with the baby boys, ten feet away on land.

OHANA

Your little sis offers you pineapple candy on the plantation train,
you all stop to feed the animals and with tortillas she sets deadly aim!
Up they fly, soaring through the sky, putting discus throwers to shame,
and when reboarding, the littlest boy sits close (nonchalance
    you feign)

Your older sister is an all-round good egg; her generosity hums in vibes,
it's always been so, but now you see that you've always been part
    of her tribe.
There's never once been a jibe, and it's not actually possible to describe
how accepting she's always been, and to her kindness we should all
    subscribe.

You recall how funny your brother is with his softly spoken voice,
and it pains you now to understand your exclusion was always a choice.
His low gruff chuckle over 'leaving Nana at the garage' tickles you pink;
the lack of concern you have reminds you you're no longer scared what
    they think.

Your mother-in-law is so much more approachable than you remember,
but it's possible that (before) you relied on 'not good enough' burning
    embers.
You have a secret talk about her previous life in Hawai'i,
and how she never thought she'd return, but being there fills her
    with glee,
and she sweetly shares her most precious commodity, delicious Earl
    Grey tea,
and you fall in line with her to quietly walk along Kukuiula quay.

KINSHIP

The delicious tang of a lilikoi doughnut soothes the busy mind,
and puka dogs and lemonade encourage you to unwind.
Red Salt breakfast tacos are immaculately designed,
and shave ice, what a thrill it is to watch the machines go griiiiind.

The family trip to the luau is an experience all its own.
A present from your sister, it's a proper show – full blown.
Hula girls, fire dancers, as the night sky fades to black,
it's painful that soon you'll leave these people, on a plane, heading back.

Now you're home and life is back to the way it's always been,
but you wonder if your life has changed as your memories convene.
You feel a part of this family (more so than ever in your life),
and how nice for that to be an added bonus, simply for marrying your wife.

So to all of you I say 'mahalo' for the proper love and care,
I honestly feel so lucky to have been part of this whole affair.

Mahalo, older sister for discarding my shyness, not giving a damn.
Mahalo, excellent sideburns for the interesting knowledge you always cram.
Mahalo, older brother for the hilarious retelling of the 'where's my pizza' scam.
Mahalo, little sister, for always accepting who I am.
Mahalo, nice husband for the Kenji suggestion – grilled cheese? Yes please! Blam!
Mahalo, teenage nephew, for snorkelling and saving my camera, woop woop, grand slam.
Mahalo, little boy, for eventually hugging me before your little butt scrammed.

OHANA

Mahalo, littlest boy, for being sweet (and having the impressive constitution of a ram).
Mahalo, baby boy, for holding my hand (your paws sticky as jam),
and mahalo to you, mother-in-law, I'm honoured to know you, ma'am.

I won't forget this trip we shared – in my veins it will ever flow,
and when I remember the trip to Koloa, it makes my beating heart glow.
I will not forget that I am a part of this family, I hope you all truly know.
And I'll cherish the memories that for ever are mine, and I say to you all:
Mahalo.

OUR FAMILY SCRAPBOOK

Erin Gannon

1. Folsom Street Fair, 1997
12B Sumner St

The circle jerk was a bust, my love. All those beefcake
postcards we strategically posted around SoMa
for nothing. Baby Blue, you with your camera.
I'm still not sure if that was a good idea.

That video of us shooting vodka is one of our great
archival moments; the wincing and the heft
of the Smirnoff bottle. It lives in the realness,
the historical feelness, of our first Folsom Street Fair.

The stilted man-on-the-street interviews
where we anticipated reality television –
and your future career. Harnessed men
signed release forms; I waited,
a celery stalk stuck in my outlaw Bloody Mary.
The autumn sunlight glistened off so much

rubber and leather, and I harassed
the executioner swinging at the public flogging.
My heckle still rings true: My dad hit me harder
with his belt. If it's that sanctified, don't put it on stage.
Folsom Street Pleasure is for everyone –
not just the whipper and the whipping boy.

> *II. Folsom Street Fair, 1997,*
> *The Hole in the Wall Saloon*

'Member that one waitress came – what was her name?
She borrowed my leather bustier and stormed
through that rubber curtain door. I never saw the thing again.
Home in the Wall. Homecoming in the Wall.

Me 'n' Cowboy Eric 'n' Eugene, we played
whatever we wanted to hear. Mainly Keith Richards.
The apex of a summer chugging cheap, warm pitchers
of cheap, warm beer. Poppers and speed

kept the back of the bar busy. I took my finals in the School
of Pissing in the Trough. There was dancing to do; you forgot
your camera back at the flat. So much dancing that day,
the heat melted the giant candle clean off the bar.

> *III. Taking Care of Business, 2000*
> *746 Geary Street, #201*

Riley told me that while I was away
they'd made a halo out of empty
beer cans in my honour. It hung from
the ceiling in the breakfast nook,
where we did our hardest working.

OUR FAMILY SCRAPBOOK

All of us were up every morning earning
to pay for the appropriate cocktail glasses,
designed for any type of cocktail
our imaginations could command.

Snifters, martinis. The ice jangled in those glasses;
all others sounded much too solidly butch. We also earned
so we could chop lines on the Bryan Ferry CD.
We called a DJ once – on KFOG! The Sounds of San Francisco.

He asked us, on the air, quite seriously,
if we'd run out of Columbian marching powder.
Riley answered in the affirmative, obviously,
with a snort. We made Night Moves –

we were American Fools. We worked
in the nook, serioso, building stamina.
Like the bug chasers we knew (and we knew them),
we chased oblivion. Our work was laden

with cackling and coughing, full of tar and gravel.
Outside, the Tenderloin sidewalks came alive
when we sang in our mouths. Full of open sores
and jangling loose change. It was all off-key,

but the work demanded delivery with maximum feeling.
I'd try on the halo, which was more like a crown.
Eventually, we'd settle down, groovy. In those days,
we put our mouths on the rocks, and when the sun came up,

they were hot, furry. We'd never remember crawling
under the blankets, curled tight against enemy alarm bells.
Riley was actually really dying, and no work was gonna set
    any of us free.

        IV. 'Wish You Were Here! Sending Irish Cock!'
        (On a Postcard Received from London, 2015)

I hold this image in my mind: four men swaying, on the other
    side of my bar,
arm in arm, singing: 'You picked a fine time to leave me,
    Lucille!'
This was my family and those were the days. Now James doesn't
    talk to anyone.
Riley's dead. David's a truck driver. You're sending me dirty
    postcards from London.

I wish I was where you are too, and what am I doing in Chicago?
It is through much melancholy I accept your offering, and I am
    grateful.

They tell me here: You're too old to wear cowboy boots.
They tell me here: Just try not to stand out so much.

You say you are going to visit, but I'm waiting and waiting.
That's some kinda purgatory, man. You know, I've never been
    that big a fan.

REBEL YELL

Jazz McCoull

Open your heart while your lover bolts for the door,
and pretend you're not sick of playing the monster.
A little costume make-up, and who can tell beauty
from the beast?
>There are no rewards
>for suffering in dignified silence, but you might as well
>for all the good crying will do you.
>The play needs its villains,
>>and haven't we always been here?

She says: 'We'll make it.'
She says: 'I'll make sure you do. Drag you through the mud
and the rain
>to a better place.'
She makes promises she can't keep,
and believes what she needs to believe. You won't hear any
argument from me. I will take love
in whatever form it is offered. I will swallow fairy tales greedily
>if they will keep me alive another day.

KINSHIP

I shrug off my ancestry, to find family and history
in people like me, forwards and back.
>Ancient and modern.
>Near and distant.
>Haven't we always been here,
>>and haven't we always loved,
>>>feared,
>>>hated,
>>>hoped
>>>as you do?

Or perhaps you don't know
>that if you cut one of us
>>we all bleed.

>There are no rewards
>for suffering in dignified silence –
>>so cry a rebel yell
>>>till your throat burns.

Please don't look at me like that. Don't look at me at all
>>if you're going to do it
>>with a sneer.
Don't you understand I'm so much more
>>than the punchline of a joke
>>at someone else's expense?

Don't you understand
that this is my world too –
>>and I will take it back from you
>>however I have to.

SITTING ON A BENCH, WAITING

Steve Denehan

I didn't know him, not really
a nod hello, the weather
he worked on the floor above
might have been five years older
it was hard to tell
what with all the weight
that he had on him
what with his face
free of wrinkles
the skin stretched taut
over jowls and chins

an enormous man
so heavy that to estimate his weight
required a five stone swing
twenty to twenty-five, or so
he smiled a lot
all teeth, a little too eager
kept himself to himself

KINSHIP

he went away one summer
two weeks, to Thailand, alone
came back married
the lads laughed about it over lunch
I saw the wedding photo on his desk
displayed proudly
she was a foot shorter
two feet narrower

years went by, another photograph appeared
a daughter, beautiful
later, another, a smiling boy
I thought about his wife
thought that this
was way above
and way beyond

I sat in the park one spring lunchtime
reading my book and eating a sandwich
he sat on a bench, waiting
I saw the light in him as they approached
his children played on the grass
he clapped his hands at their awful cartwheels
his wife looked at him
slipped her hand into his
I got back to my book and left them to it

SITTING ON YOUR BED

Ginger

I used to sit on your bed
and dream of the day
I'd be your mother.

Well, it wasn't technically your bed then.
We were part-way through
the adoption process

in the bizarre stage
of having ourselves
and our home assessed

so our 'spare rooms'
were now children's rooms,
despite being childless.

We'd chosen neutral colours
so you could
make them your own.

KINSHIP

We'd put some removable transfers
on the walls that could peel off
if not to your taste,

and snuck a couple of pink pictures
on to one of the blue wardrobes,
balancing ingrained ideas of girl and boy.

I sat on your bed
many times
through the years

trying, without much success
to get you to sleep
so that you could rest and so could I.

But it's hard to sleep
when you've been removed from your home
in the middle of the night

by police and social workers,
in your Paddington Bear pyjamas,
never to return.

You grew
and the duvet covers changed
though the determination and the toy cat did not.

I've sat on your bed in recent years,
trying to get you
to see my point of view,

SITTING ON YOUR BED

but teenagers have
their own rules
and ours seem outdated.

Besides, when you've had to
parent yourself,
it's hard to let another step in.

I sat on your bed
today, when you left
to start your new life.

University, a new town,
new friends to live with,
a world to explore.

I didn't know your earliest years
and tried to fill in the gaps
by things you said when little,

sitting on your bed,
trying to interpret and soothe
your memories and nightmares.

Now we've come full circle
and the gaps are now full of new things
you don't want to share with us.

I hope we've filled you
full of love
to bridge the gaps.

KINSHIP

Stay safe, my little grown-up girl,
come back and share your adventures
and we'll sit on your bed once more.

STYX

For Grandpa

Jayant Kashyap

You always forgot where the bus station was,
where your slippers were –

I'm going there, you'd say,
yet you didn't need to and you never went.

We'd almost always collect you from somewhere else,
and the times when you came home

yourself, you'd have been to someone's farm
and you'd have called it somewhere else;

you weren't a Google Maps person, either –
you were more a bird losing sight of his nest

slowly
and then we lost you.

KINSHIP

And people from your English classes came
to see you; to say goodbye;

everyone had their way of paying respects –
some sat by your body on ice for hours and wept

endlessly; some waited at your pyre
as you learnt to be free.

Your leaving's been sad, even after years,

but you're in a better place now, they've said.

We keep finding your slippers every day;
the bus station is still just as far.

TEETH REMOVAL CAN BE FUN, SOMETIMES

Rush Day

i use a melonballer to remove
your teeth from the inside of my
wrist and give them to the man
in front of us. he wears them around
his neck and tells our fortune with
them. old maids, he says, you will be
old maids, withered and die alone and
probably unloved. and we laugh like we
do, always, tear our throats with it and
stain our ankles with the mud we brave
as we walk away. old, withered and probably
unloved. we will sit in our kitchen at two
a.m. and i will watch you peel pomegranates
with the tip of your orange fingernails and
pretend that the red staining your fingers
is the blood of the men who told us our hands
would never be sacred. old, withered and probably unloved.
there's always a taco bell open when we're together.

KINSHIP

the walls around us aren't thick enough to contain
the laughter that rips from us. old, withered
and probably unloved. at least we won't
end up on tv, pretending to be loved,
at least we won't end up as bollywood
wives, you will say and i will laugh,
because at least we made it out before
they killed us. there is only so much
laughter we can give before the floors
get stale with it. there is only so much
laughter we can take before our hands shake
with it. old, withered and probably unloved. i
will use a melonballer to remove my
teeth from the inside of your wrist and
laugh when there's no man in front
of us to take them.

THE OLD MAN AND THE VIOLIN

Catherine Edmunds

They are teaching me to play violin,
but my fingers have been broken too often.
I tell the doctor. He pretends to take notes.
I think that perhaps his wife is leaving him,
and listening to me helps him to understand
how there are worse things
that can happen to a man.

I am half asleep by the fire,
remembering my mother and father dancing,
my uncle playing violin.

They've given me this Made in China violin.
I think the Chinese people do not sit
in a friendly workshop and lovingly craft
this thing. I think they work ugly shifts
and sleep in ugly cells to send pennies back
to villages where children grow up
not knowing their parents.

KINSHIP

When I draw the bow,
I hear screaming and burning –
my mother weeping, my father's limbs shattered.

The teacher's violin rattles.
A shoulder is loose.
I offer to mend it, but he hears something else.
I see his fear.
My hand curls into a fist. I have killed,
but not with malice. I have hated,
but only the act of killing.

We play 'Twinkle, Twinkle Little Star',
a simple melody, for a child.
It is the village we burnt,
it is the orphans we forced to march on ahead.

I would like to repair the teacher's violin.
I would like to fall asleep beside the fire,
my mother and father dancing.

The class is over. I stay behind,
play my memories, sub voce,
and when I finally look up,
the teacher sees me for the first time.
I think he is crying, but not with sorrow.
He gets out his own violin,
and plays me his little son's favourite song.
I know this tune!

I tell him, I can fix that rattle.
I think he will let me now.

THE SINGER

Niam Moore

I remember you at your Singer.
Oversized denim shirt with pearl snap fasteners.
Mouthful of pins and needles. Periodic whirring rattling its way around, vibrations bouncing off walls and eardrums.
Your foot depressing the black pedal and rising again.
Up and down.
Up. and. down.
Up. and. down.
Sometimes rhythmic, tide-like. Often not. Often lengthy gaps where you picked at mistakes.
Snipped threads.
Readjusted fabric.
Reset reels.
Or called me to tackle the duties of a dressmaker's dummy.
Niam!
I arrive to a stiff neck and perhaps a stiffer garment.
Asked to stand this way and that.
Pinched, pricked and prodded. My usefulness expires.
Sunlight dwindles. A glowing lamp emerges.

KINSHIP

I remember you at your Singer.
Mouthful of bun and cheese. Periodic groaning rattling its way around, vibrations bouncing off walls and eardrums.
Your foot depressing the black pedal and rising again.
Up. and. down.
Up. and. down.
Up and down.
Never rhythmic. You stab at mistakes.
Chew threads.
Rip fabrics.
Launch reels.
Finally calling me to tackle the duties of a dressmaker's dummy.
Niam!!!
I arrive to a stiff neck and weary smile.
A shirt for school.
I remember you at your Singer.

WE PICTURED IT SUNNY

Naomi Dean

We pictured it sunny,
like usual, planned for
a picnic. Middle of May,
Syttende Mai, we'd be thawed
out from winter, taking the
warmth and the green as our
comfort. It was a Sunday,
so we'd bring our kids, linger
graveside over sandwiches
and coffee, Swedish toast
and banana cream pie.

There would be no letting up,
a dozen years (!) to the day.
The Norway maple is the slightest
of refuge. We take it anyway,
repeating the stories, wishing
we could add new ones.
You're driving to school,
coffee in one hand, cigarette

KINSHIP

in the other, playing hooky
to watch *General Hospital* and
sunbathe, while we talk of you.

We pass around the brownies,
quarantined in tin foil, in hopes
we don't pass around the plague.
Our umbrellas nudge us to keep
our distance, but we lean in at
the good parts. This isn't the year for
sprawling on lawn chairs in the sun.
It's for mucking up tennis shoes,
standing in sadness, drawing
raincoats closer and lasting
an hour in our remembering.

WHEN YOU WERE

(*BEFORE I WAS*)

Vijaya Venkatesan

I have seated them in the shady part of the garden where sunlight paints filigree on their skin. Hands flick-flack, punctuate the bounce-skip-jump as they play hopscotch with languages, shriek, whoop and laugh. I fill indulgent bowls with snacks, rinse out the goose-necked glass jug.

The resolutely black-haired one bobs her head towards her sister – Remember when the gardener's boy found you smoking a cheroot and you called him a bloody fool? The older sister groans, Aiyoh, claps appalled hands to her face. They recite the rosary of tram stops from school: Mahlwagon, Upper Pazundaung Road, Merchant Street, Sule Pagoda Road, Dalhousie Street, Strand Road, Kemmendine Road, Shan Road, Kemmendine, Hanthawaddy.

They switch to Burmese often and lose me. The voice of their childhood, the language their younger selves carried into exile, scant possessions in hasty bundles. Do you remember the Kemmendine house, asks someone. They invoke memories of the house and its grounds in Burmese; the occasional 'mango trees' or 'cricket bat' poke through in English.

I don't feel left out. They have told me these stories rubbed and polished in other languages. I lift the laden tray, step out into the sunlight. I dream of the house every night, my mother says softly. In English to her sister, brother, and an assortment cousins seated in the shade. My happiest days. The ice cubes in the jug shiver. Before me, yes, that you're allowed, yes to unlimited happiness before me. But since me, happiest days even since me? Could you not have said that in Burmese, Amma? I say none of this aloud.

XUĚLÓU, HÉNÁN 2021

Mea Andrews

Swallows dip low to the ground, hug invisible
curve, insect hungry. An old woman more
skeleton than skin tosses round sesame bread,
insides coated with salt, for people
ordering them in threes. I order five to share.

Today we go to my husband's hometown,
a prison village where his yéyé was a guard,
while his parents sold fruits in Beijing.
He's called back to an abandoned pile of bricks
over two hundred prisoners used to share,
tile roof red-brown broken. His childhood
home already torn down. A white rectangle,
his old one classroom school, little gold-
star flag out front.

Four kids sit on a broken pedestal of rocks,
watch our car roll by, forgetting us as
we pass. Husband fingers once upon
a time ponds, now sloping corn stalks.
The road ends in dirt and grass, so we walk,

KINSHIP

greeted by a dog with ears like an oversized
bat and hip bones junting off his sides.
He barks when I move, growls when I turn
my back to him, whines when husband
does the same.

An old man eyes my skin – too light – husband
calls out to him, greets him as shūshu and I fade
into the background as they half embrace, arms
around backs but faces forward. I ask if
it's really his uncle, but he is lost to me. He's running
rocks between his heels and the ground, pouring
water into lost ponds, fishing with shū
not shū, grandfather haunting his shoulder.

YOU (A PUDDLE)

Tom Chachewitz

You told me
that you were

           a puddle of

oil,
meaningless in your muddiness.

I told you that in every drop

           of us

there's a prism of colours,
reflecting our true form.

ABOUT THE POETS

ROSALIE ALSTON *p. 55*

Rosalie Alston grew up in the Essex countryside, and now lives in Bristol, where she enjoys the community poetry scene, which is diverse and vibrant, with so many supportive poets. She has had poems published online and in print, including in *Spelt* and *Black Lives Matter: Poems for a New World*. A number of her published poems are about adoption and fostering, and a poem about moving between foster homes was Highly Commended in a *Poetry Space* competition. She is thrilled to be in *Kinship* with this poem about friendship and family.

MEA ANDREWS *p. 125*

Mea Andrews is a writer from Georgia, who currently resides in Hong Kong. She has just finished her MFA from Lindenwood University, and is only recently back on the publishing scene. You can find her in *Gordon Square Review*, *Rappahannock Review*, *Tipton Poetry Journal*, *Potomac Review* and others.

STEVE BAGGS *p. 45*

Steve Baggs is a poet and writer from Kent. Born in Deal, he now lives in Canterbury. He has been published in several poetry magazines and is putting together his first collection of poetry. He has previously won a Co-Op Poetry Festival prize, and has performed his poetry across the country. He was once arrested for an impromptu poetry reading as part of a teenage guerrilla poetry night.

Thankfully, it was all a misunderstanding! He enjoys writing haiku and has contributed to the *Time Haiku* magazine, and recently won second prize for a haibun he wrote.

CAROLINE BRACKEN *p. 17*

Caroline Bracken is an Irish poet living in Dublin. Her poems have been published in *Poetry Wales*, *Poetry News* (Poetry Society UK), *New England Review*, the *Irish Times*, *The North*, *Poetry Jukebox*, *Gutter Magazine*, *Belfield Literary Review*, *Erbacce Journal*, *Howl* and *Best New British & Irish Poets 2019–2021*. She was shortlisted in the Manchester Poetry Prize 2020 and the Alpine Fellowship Prize 2022.

TOM CHACHEWITZ *p. 127*

Tom Chachewitz (also published as Tom Stockley) is a queer punk poet living and working across south-west England. A self-taught writer and performer, they cut their teeth on DIY punk gigs and community theatre and have since written and produced work for BBC Arts, UNESCO and the Tate. They were shortlisted for the 2023 Outspoken Prize for Poetry and have been published by Bloomsbury, Perennial Press, Sassify, Ample Press, Queerlings and HUCK. Their debut collection *Back to the Fuchsia* is due to be published by Arkbound Press in 2024.

JUNYI CHEW *p. 59*

Junyi Chew currently resides on the outer edge of Leeds, having previously lived in Mexico, Brazil and Spain, and grown up in Kent in a Malaysian-Chinese family. She often explores liminal spaces in her writing, such as the experience of being between cultures, or between waking and dreaming, but this featured poem, 'Earthstruck', describes the profound feeling of kinship between all nations and species that has been described by astronauts on their first glimpse of our planet from space.

MICHÈLE CLEMENT *p. 23*

Michèle Clement is a retired Consultant Dermatologist with two amazing sons and daughters-in-law and four wonderful grandchildren. She lives with her Civil Partner, Stephanie, and a naughty black Cocker Spaniel, Leo. Michèle was born in Nairobi, Kenya, returning to England to go to boarding school in 1962. Her parents followed and subsequently lived in both England and Malta. The concept of home has intrigued her all her life – she has had many houses, but is not sure where home is. Her heart remains in Kenya, which cannot be her home.

RUSH DAY *p. 115*

Rush is twenty-two years old and studies English at the University of St Andrews. They have two dogs. They are deeply fond of Old English poetry and Midwestern American poetry and Midwestern horror.

NAOMI DEAN *p. 121*

Naomi Dean grew up on a farm in Minnesota. She has taught English and Spanish in Brooklyn, New York and Palo Alto, California. She currently teaches English as a Second Language to students at a public elementary school in the Twin Cities, Minnesota, where she lives with her husband, son and daughter. Naomi's work has recently appeared in *Poetica, Sylvia, The Madrigal, NiftyLit, Collateral, Plainsongs, JAMA* and *Medmic*.

STEVE DENEHAN *p. 107*

Steve Denehan lives in Kildare, Ireland with his wife Eimear and daughter Robin. He is the author of two chapbooks and four poetry collections, most recently *As If It Meant Something*, published by Renard Press in 2023. Winner of the Anthony Cronin Poetry Award and twice winner of the *Irish Times*' New Irish Writing, his numerous publication credits include *Poetry Ireland Review* and *Westerly*.

M.A. DUBBS *p. 73*

M.A. Dubbs is an award-winning Mexican-American and LGBT poet from Indiana. For over a decade, Dubbs has published writing in magazines and anthologies across the globe. She is the author of the chapbook *An American Mujer*, and served as a judge for Indiana's Poetry Out Loud Competition. She recently won the 2023 Holden Vaughn Spangler Award from River City College MUSE. When not writing, Dubbs likes to pretend that she is a 90s anime magical girl.

A.W. EARL *p. 85*

A.W. Earl is a poet, novelist and storyteller. They studied English Literature with Creative Writing at the University of East Anglia and hold an MA in Medieval and Early Modern Textual Cultures. They have written for the LGBTQ+ crowdfunding platform Pride Pocket, and their work has appeared in *Bloodbath Literary Zine*, *Lighthouse Journal* and *The Selkie*. They were a judge for The Dracula Society's 2021 Children of the Night Award. *Time's Fool*, their debut novel, was published by Unbound in 2018.

ABOUT THE POETS

CATHERINE EDMUNDS *p. 117*

Catherine Edmunds is a writer, portrait artist and professional violinist. Her published works include two poetry collections, five novels and a Holocaust memoir, as well as numerous short stories and poems in journals including *Aesthetica*, *Crannóg* and *Ambit*. She has been nominated three times for a Pushcart Prize, shortlisted for the Bridport Prize four times, and was the 2020 winner of the Robert Graves Poetry Prize. Catherine is married and lives in historic Bishop Auckland, in the foothills of the Pennines in the north of England.

RENEE EMERSON *p. 61*

Renee Emerson is the author of the poetry collections *Keeping Me Still*, *Threshing Floor* and *Church Ladies*, the chapbook *The Commonplace Misfortunes of Everyday Plants* and the middle grade novel *Why Silas Miller Must Learn to Ride a Bike*. She lives in the Midwest with her husband and five children.

NAOISE GALE *p. 63*

Naoise Gale is a poet from West Yorkshire who writes about mental illness and addiction. She was runner-up in the AUB International Poetry Prize 2023, and first-prize winner of the Ledbury Poetry Competition 2022. Her debut pamphlet *After the Flood Comes the Apologies* was longlisted for the Poetry Book Awards 2023, and was described in *Buzz Mag* as 'gritty and gorgeous'. Naoise is currently studying an MA in Creative Writing Poetry at the University of East Anglia, and is working on her first full-length collection. In her spare time she enjoys baking.

KINSHIP

ERIN GANNON *p. 101*

Erin Gannon is a poet, singer and biker chick. Her practice meanders between verse, music and performance. She has been published in *Honest Ulsterman*, *Gutter Magazine*, the BMF's *Rider Magazine* and elsewhere. She holds an MA in Poetry from Queen's University, Belfast and is finishing her doctoral thesis in Creative Writing at the University of Glasgow.

DEBORAH GAUDIN *p. 77*

Deborah Gaudin is a Pantheist poet, living on the Welsh Marches, whose connection to the land informs her outlook and writing. Her love of poetry began at an early age, listening to her father recite poetry. Deborah is currently working on a couple of collections of poetry, and has in the past, with the help of her husband, produced two collections on CD. As a long-time member of Border Poets, she has been inspired and exposed to a wide variety of styles. She has been published in Border Poet anthologies, as well as in independent magazines.

JEAN GILLESPIE *p. 41*

Jean Gillespie is a visual artist and poet. She was brought up in a rural mining village in West Lothian, near the iconic Forth Rail Bridge. Jean started writing in 2020 during lockdown and has continued with a passion ever since. She enjoys taking her poetry to open-mic nights in Edinburgh, and is working on merging her poems and artwork together; she has exhibited these in Kyoto, Japan and at the Tatha Gallery in Scotland. She is currently exhibiting at the City Arts Centre in Edinburgh.

ABOUT THE POETS

GINGER *p. 109*

Ginger has loved poetry ever since discovering Dr Seuss's *Yertle the Turtle* in childhood. She adores reading, writing, listening to and performing poetry and prose and was delighted to enrol on an English degree and go to university in her late forties. She was less delighted when the pandemic meant she had to shield for over half of the degree, but still had an amazing time studying remotely with her fantastic fellow students and wonderful lecturers. She gained a First and was able to stop shielding in time for the most brilliant graduation day ever!

BENEDICT HANGIRIZA *p. 49*

Benedict Hangiriza's works are published or upcoming in *Tint Journal*, *Bacopa Literary Review*, *Afritondo*, *Spare Parts Lit*, *Swim Press*, *The Kalahari Review* and *Writers Space Africa*. He lives in Kampala, Uganda.

OZ HARDWICK *p. 81*

Oz is a resolutely European poet, whose work has been widely published in international journals and anthologies. He has published quite a few full collections and chapbooks, including *Learning to Have Lost*, which won the 2019 Rubery International Book Award for poetry, and, most recently, *A Census of Preconceptions*. Oz has held residencies in the UK, Europe, the US and Australia, and has performed internationally at major festivals and in run-down bars. Oz is Professor of Creative Writing at Leeds Trinity University.

ROISÍN HARKIN *p. 43*

Roisín Harkin is a mother of four young children, originally from the Inishowen Peninsula in Co. Donegal, Ireland, and now living in Solihull, West Midlands. An arts graduate of the University of Ulster, Roisín is currently taking time out from her career in the corporate world to focus on raising her children, and, when not being asked for a snack, to write poetry.

ELLIE HERDA-GRIMWOOD　　　　　　　　　　　　　　*p. 95*

Ellie is delighted to be now thrice(!) published with Renard Press, and thanks them very much for rewarding her jumbly thoughts. Ohana (the Hawaiian term for 'family') has become increasingly important as she slowly ages into an inevitably salty hag and she appreciates those closest to her more and more. She is a very proud aunt to multiple niblings with another tiny girl due soon. She credits her mama and papa for their eternal encouragement and support – she wouldn't be where she is without them – and her gorgeous wife for everything else, always.

SRISHTI JAIN　　　　　　　　　　　　　　　　　　　*p. 33*

Srishti Jain is an Indian poet and medical writer based in Sydney. Her poems are forthcoming in the 2023 *Ros Spencer* and *The Aleph Review* anthologies. Her work has previously been published in various journals including *The Seattle Star*, *Red Ogre Review*, *Rigorous*, *The Cancer Researcher*, *Meniscus* and *Clepsydra – Literary and Art Magazine*. Her poetry on climate justice can be found in the streets of Dublin as part of The Bohemian Way campaign.

CONNOR JOHNSTON　　　　　　　　　　　　　　　　*p. 29*

Connor Johnston is a poet and writer currently undertaking an MPhil in English Studies at Wolfson College, Cambridge. He is studying Victorian queerness in particular, and has an interest

ABOUT THE POETS

in writing both traditional and modern poems (inspired by his favourite poet, Gerard Manley Hopkins), as well as fantasy novels (inspired by his favourite novelist, Ursula K. Le Guin).

MARIYAM KAROLIA *p. 83*

Mariyam Karolia is a deaf poet and storyteller from Bradford. Recently selected by the Genesis Foundation as a 2023 Emerging Writer, she has been shortlisted a number of times for poetry and short stories. As a care leaver she is hoping to change the narrative about the care system.

JAYANT KASHYAP *p. 113*

Jayant Kashyap, a poet, essayist, translator and artist, has published two pamphlets and a zine, *Water*. His work appears in *POETRY*, *Magma*, *Poetry Wales* and elsewhere.

BEK KING *p. 35*

Bek is a keen writer currently undergoing an English Literature with Creative Writing BA at Newcastle University. Her work is often inspired by the 'Others' of society, which she explores through writing historical playscripts. When she writes poetry, it often concerns conflict between religion, gender and sexuality, reflecting her experience of being raised in a high-demand religion. She loves penguins, and is a big Isabella Whitney enthusiast.

JESSIE LEE *p. 37*

Born and raised in London, Jessie Lee is a British-Chinese writer with a particular focus on experimental format and identity. She graduated from the University of Leeds with a BA in English and Comparative Literature, and spends her time writing poetry and reading about hope. She is a lover of love, the good in humanity, ice cream on cold days and women.

CAOIMHE MATTHEWS *p. 39*

Caoimhe Matthews was born and raised in Dundalk, Ireland, but unfortunately currently lives in the UK. She gets excited when she sees squirrels, even though she sees them every day. She's always worried that people are mad at her. Her grandmother kept a framed photo of her in the sitting room, where she is a toddler and is wearing multiple layers of rosary beads. Her favourite graffiti from her hometown was at the local bus depot; it said 'Tupac Was Here'. He was not.

JAZZ MCCOULL *p. 105*

Jazz McCoull is a non-binary writer born and based in the north of England. Their work primarily examines themes of identity, embodiment and transformation through a lens of nature and spirituality. They previously appeared in 2022's *Spectrum* anthology from Renard Press, and *OUCH! Collective's* second volume, released in 2023.

DIANNE MCPHELIM *p. 19*

Born in Australia, Dianne McPhelim lives in beautiful rural Ireland. Having recently graduated with a BA in Writing and Literature from ATU Sligo, she is currently studying for an MA in Modern Literature and working on an anthology.

FEDORA MENSAH *p. 91*

Based in the quiet suburb of Chafford Hundred, Thurrock, Fedora Mensah is an avid reader with a love for foreign films and a weakness for indulging in too much chocolate for

ABOUT THE POETS

her own good. When she is not studying (which is rarely!) or creating new calligraphy designs for her business (which is also rarely!), you can find her slowly but surely drafting another poetry book.

NIAM MOORE *p. 119*

London born, Hackney based writer Niam narrates his experience of class, race and loss through his novels, scripts and poetry. Themes of failure, growing up in inner London and the existential dread of forgetting his late mother fill the pages of his work and echo throughout his vibrant spoken-word performances. Niam tells his stories with a natural flow, weaving striking tales that are trying, uplifting and self-reportedly humorous.

INGA PIOTROWSKA *p. 69*

Inga Piotrowska is a Polish poet currently living in Manchester. Her first poetry book was published in Poland in 2018, and she was shortlisted for the Bridport Prize in 2023. Her English poetry was chosen to be published in *harana poetry*, *Wild Roof Journal*, *Eye to the Telescope*, *Thimble Lit* and others.

ILISHA THIRU PURCELL *p. 51*

Ilisha Thiru Purcell is a poet based in and from Newcastle upon Tyne. Ilisha is one of the three poets in the inaugural cohort of the Poets of Colour Incubator, and is a Young Creative Associate with New Writing North. Ilisha won a commission to perform at the 2023 Newcastle Poetry Festival, and was selected to be part of Apples and Snakes' development programme Word's a Stage 2.0. Her work has appeared in publications such as *Popshot*, *The Butcher's Dog* and *Dear Damsels*, and she is a member of the collective Brown Girls Write.

IVY RAFF *p. 21*

Ivy Raff is the author of *What Remains / Qué queda* (bilingual English/Spanish edition forthcoming 2023), winner of the Alberola International Poetry Prize, and *Rooted and Reduced to Dust* (forthcoming 2024), hailed by Bruce Smith as 'lacerating, fearless.' Individual poems appear in *The American Journal of Poetry*, Electric Literature's *The Commuter*, *Nimrod International Journal* and *West Trade Review*, among numerous others, as well as in Renard's 2022 anthology *Spectrum: Poetry Celebrating Identity*. Her *Best of the Net*-nominated work has garnered scholarship support from the Colgate Writers Conference, the Hudson Valley Writers Center and Under the Volcano.

DAPHNE SAMPSON *p. 65*

Born in north London, Daphne started reading poetry as a moon-struck teenager. She grew up in Kent, where her botanist father enjoyed growing trees from seed. Subsequently she worked in two wonderfully creative primary schools off the Old Kent Road, previously only known to her as that brown Monopoly card, the cheapest on the board. This vibrant community had some of the exhilaration of the first plunge of a wild swim. She taught for two years in Kenya, which further nourished her love of nature. Later in Norfolk with her young family Daphne became involved in environmental campaigning.

KAY SAUNDERS *p. 79*

Kay Saunders is a young woman from the Cotswolds who has been writing creatively her whole life. A core source of

ABOUT THE POETS

her inspiration has come from her experiences as someone within the LGBT+ community, which empowers her to create heartfelt narratives that are relatable and a safe place for people to feel seen and understood. Between short stories, flash fiction and poetry, Kay has won local awards for her writing and recognition from publishers and authors, and hopes to soon join her literary idols in a world of publication as she works on her first novel.

THEA SMILEY *p. 57*

Thea Smiley is a Suffolk-based poet. Her poems have been shortlisted for the Bridport Prize and Live Canon Collection competition, longlisted in the Rialto Nature and Place competition, commended in the Hippocrates Prize, Poets and Players and Ware Poets competitions, and published in anthologies and magazines including *The Alchemy Spoon*, *Finished Creatures* and *Butcher's Dog*.

ALYSON SMITH *p. 89*

Alyson Smith works as an administrator in a Nursing Home in Newcastle upon Tyne. Alongside this she has recently completed an MA in Creative Writing though the Open University, and is working on her first collection of short stories. Alyson has a long-standing Bipolar diagnosis and a recent diagnosis of Level 1 Autism, which has helped her to understand why she doesn't always see the world as others do.

SAM SZANTO *p. 75*

Sam Szanto lives in Durham. She is a poetry and prose writer, and an editor at *The Afterpast Review*. Her collaborative pamphlet, *Splashing Pink* was recently published by Hedgehog

Press, and is a Poetry Book Society Winter 2023 Pamphlet Choice. She won the 2020 Charroux Poetry Prize and the First Writer International Poetry Prize. Her poetry has been accepted for publication in journals including *The North*, *Northern Gravy* and *The Storms*. Her story collection *If No One Speaks* was published by Alien Buddha Press in 2022.

ELIZABETH TRAIN-BROWN *p. 71*

Elizabeth Train-Brown is a twice-shortlisted Poet of the Year whose debut collection, *salmacis: becoming not quite a woman*, was published by Renard Press in 2022. Using Greek myth as metaphor for gender exploration, Elizabeth's collection was hailed by critics as a 'a beautifully lyrical debut collection with real power in its pages' (*Debut Digest*). 'Hades' is a poem about love and community but particularly that space where the two don't always fit, told through a reimagining of the original Hades and Persephone myth. It forms part of Elizabeth's upcoming collection, *where the womb wandered*, exploring the vulnerable side of history's men.

UTSUK UPRETI *p. 87*

Utsuk Upreti is a recent graduate from St Xavier's College, Maitighar whose heart has always been captivated by the magic of storytelling. According to his mother, as a child, he would often be found nestled in a quiet corner of a room, lost in his thoughts, and would exclaim, if asked, 'I'm thinking of a story!' Through film, short stories and poems, Utsuk seeks to transform an idea, as personal as it might be, and survive by expressing and knowing himself in this challenging, unforgiving world.

ABOUT THE POETS

VIJAYA VENKATESAN *p. 123*

Born and raised in India, Vijaya Venkatesan went to university in the UK. She has an LL.M in International Law from Cambridge University and has spent her professional life in the public sector. She has been longlisted for the National Poetry Competition and won the Charm Poetry competition. The abiding love of her life is Liverpool Football Club. She lives in London.

ANNE MARIE WELLS *p. 25*

Anne Marie Wells is an award-winning queer poet, playwright and memoirist navigating the world with a chronic illness. She is the author of *Survived By*, *Happy Iceland* and *Mother, (v)* and is an accomplished copywriter, editor and poetry instructor who has supported dozens of authors in publishing their manuscripts.

STUART WRIGLEY *p. 53*

Originally from Prescot, a village just outside Liverpool, Stuart has studied Applied Linguistics and History, and is just a few more biros away from completing a PhD in history. He teaches aspiring and inspiring young people at Royal Holloway, University of London. Poetry and running are vital aspects in Stuart's life; they happen when he's not studying or teaching.

There were originally another four poems on the shortlist, but sadly we were unable to include their work in this anthology.

SUPPORTERS

This project was made possible through the financial support of the kind people listed below (in alphabetical order).

Sharmishta Chatterjee-Banerjee
Michèle Clement
Chris and Joanna Cooke
Steve Denehan
A.W. Earl
Janet Fearnley
Deborah Gaudin
Ellie Herda-Grimwood
Peter Hill
Matt Leonard
Tevye Markson
Cheryl Moore
Ilisha Thiru Purcell
Shelly Reed Thieman
and Anonymous